MW01592175

With In

by Janine Mary Stefanucci-Hexter

DORRANCE
PUBLISHING CO
EST. 1920
PITTSBURGH, PENNSYLVANIA 15238

The contents of this work, including, but not limited to, the accuracy of events, people, and places depicted; opinions expressed; permission to use previously published materials included; and any advice given or actions advocated are solely the responsibility of the author, who assumes all liability for said work and indemnifies the publisher against any claims stemming from publication of the work.

All Rights Reserved
Copyright © 2016 by Janine Mary Stefanucci-Hexter

No part of this book may be reproduced or transmitted, downloaded, distributed, reverse engineered, or stored in or introduced into any information storage and retrieval system, in any form or by any means, including photocopying and recording, whether electronic or mechanical, now known or hereinafter invented without permission in writing from the publisher.

Dorrance Publishing Co
585 Alpha Drive
Suite 103
Pittsburgh, PA 15238
Visit our website at www.dorrancebookstore.com

ISBN: 978-1-4809-1866-5
eISBN: 978-1-4809-1843-6

Contents

Dedication vii
Inspirations ix
Acknowledgments xi

Part 1: Poems
Addiction 3
Adore 4
Afraid 5
A Friend 6
Angelina 7
A Peek 8
Behind Closed Doors 10
Blamed 11
Blind 12
Born 13
Bounce 14
Caged 15
Cleansed 16
Christmas Snow 17
Clouds 18
Crooked 19
Crutch 20
Decision 21
Desperate 22
Diseased 24
Disguise 25
Don't Doubt 26
Everyone 27
Family 28
Flying 29
Free? 30
Freeze 31
Gentlemen's Day Care Center 32
Granddad 33
Grandmoms 34
Halloween 35

Hold onto the Sky 36
How Do I? 37
Hungry 38
Let The Butterflies Fly 39
Loving 40
Met 41
Midnight 42
Mirrors 43
Mommy Dearest 44
Misunderstood 45
Money Spell 46
My Angel 47
My Teddy Bear 48
Near 49
Neglected 50
Once upon a Dream 51
Pool 52
Progressed 54
Promised 56
Punishment 57
Push 58
Rescue Me 59
Rewind 60
See 61
Sneaky 62
Shining Faces 63
Subject Eyes 65
Sweet Winds 67
Survivor 68
The Crow 69
The Hawk 70
The Lucky Pen 71
The Night 72
The Rings 73
The Spell 74
The Walk 75

Tides 76
Tongues 77
To the Heaven's 78
Tourist 79
Trees 80
Truth 82
Tunes 83
Waiting 84
Where? 85
Why Not Me? 88
Without You 91

Part 2: Song Lyrics
Because of You 95
Heartache to Heartache 97
Hearts Individually 99
Heaven Falls 101
Lost for Words 104
Rip It 107
Shared 109

Dedication

I dedicate this book to my family and to Edgar Allen Poe. What was he really thinking when that pen hit the paper? In some of my ideas, I want you to wonder also.

I also dedicate this book to all my fans, and again, family and friends, and my promoter, for pushing me to my dream as it's coming true. I've worked really hard on this book.

Thanks, Jesus!

Inspirations

I was so inspired by Jesus and the words of the Bible, dictionaries, thesaurus, and music; by nature, other people's stories, old loved ones, and events of sorrow and grace in my life; and by the creation and imagination of my mind and dreams. The truth that shall set you free.

Acknowledgments

Thank you again, the Success Center and the Mt. Holly Library in Mt. Holly, NJ. They didn't plant me a tree yet, but when they do, I hope there's money at the top to donate for what was given to me. I thank the Lord for this gift.

Thank you, and God bless.

See you soon.

Part 1: Poems

Addiction

It calls me twenty-four hours a day and seven days a week.
It constantly crawls in my mind.
A second sometimes is too much.
How do I put the progressing behind?

Sobriety brings the past memories.
Quitting is the easy part.
As your body and mind returns,
The reasons come back to the start.

So vulnerable, so easy to go back,
thinking it's the easier way out,
Then I started opening my mouth.

I want to change. Unknown it is.
I never even got to be a kid.
I want to make the right decisions and
trust myself and forgive.

I've been abused and used, and I did too.
I need Jesus and N.A.,
to walk me through.

You died for my sins.
Please don't let me go back, where I've been.

In the beginning, you feel weak.
You have to pray and give each second to God!
As your strengths arrive,
the world will still turn as you try to survive.

Stay away from people, places, and things.
Fight for your freedom eternally, in sobriety.

Adore

Adorable in every way.
No kitten could ever take her place.
She gives you love in every way.
She listens when you say.
She plays with her own invention of games.
Pearl is her name.
She cuddles with you every night and
peeks to see if you're still in sight.
She eats when you eat.
She watches TV with you.
I spoil her with love and she spreads it to you.
She never runs out the door,
because she knows where she is adored.

Afraid

I use to walk the streets only at night,
Thinking this was the peace of life.

Stars, the moon, the silence everywhere.
Then I didn't hear the sounds of children, whom I don't have around.
Walking in the dare,
Only trouble to be found.

The one to hide from life would only come out at night.
It no longer gave me fright.

I always had to hide,
Just hoping to make it
home to get again high.

Now it's jails, institutions, and death to face.
As the night crawls,
I'm now afraid.

Now learning not to be afraid of the day.
Life is so hard.
I have to learn to not hide away,
so I won't be just a card.

A Friend

You never know who you'll meet,
Another book to read inside
and be swept off your feet.

Someone who, from the beginning till
the end, never leaves your side and
walks you through the laughter and the cries.

Trueness of the heart and
never afraid to be.
Someone you always trust,
and you can be open to help you positively.

Never just thinks of themselves and
teaches us the best of ourselves.

A love develops instantly, stronger in time.
Sharing openly with beauty and desires,
creating moments within binds.

Never leaving each other's side,
through the travel of each other's lives,
a carriage for all triumphs and trials.

And most of all,
loving them unconditionally.
If you need a friend, write me.

Angelina

I see her every night.
She still tucks me in tight.
She's such a beautiful sight.
She still keeps me right and alive.

She practically raised me.
She brought out the good in me.
I couldn't ever wait to see
her again, for there always was a treat.

I wish she was still here today.
I'd hug and kiss her still to this day.
I would still be able to play.
I wonder what she now would say?

As Heaven grants me this sight,
every single night,
she still is my light.
I hope she continues to
tuck me in at night.

And when my time arrives,
I hope I see her in the Jesus' lights.
I miss and love you so much.
Thank you for never leaving my side.

A Peek

I had to take a peek, without thoughts of consequences
in a life fenced in.

I put lust and danger together,
not even knowing his cover.

The moment was raised by me,
a simple quest to kiss me?

I did not know this would stay with me.
His thoughts never did proceed.

So why do I cry, he might want to know?
Sympathy never shone.

I risked my marriage.
He risked his life.
I am still a wife.

I know now he'll avoid me.
He can't handle the company.

Now I'm hurt that I peeked.
A new life to be seeked?

Now I have to leave him alone.
He wants to be alone.

I did ask for another peek.
The kind of sex, no one speaks,

but if I can't stop crying over a kiss,
imagine what would of happened if we blissed?

I felt something I can't take away.
Now he's gone away.

No matter if married or not,
he admitted it would not be.
Now I have to ignore the peek.
The one he wants to be with is not me.

Behind Closed Doors

He is the funniest man you'll ever meet and
works hard and neat.
He'd help anyone.
He helped me.
Situations were twisted,
two different minds.
I married him and we intertwined,
growing, learning, understanding at queue.
Now behind closed doors,
You're no longer you.
When the doors close and we're all alone,
I feel I'm in a jail trapped in your sad world.
I'm no longer happy.
I'm just rolled up in a curl
in tears 'cause I don't understand.
Where is my man?
You stopped to understand.
Now all I have is Jesus' hands.
We use to laugh; now we yell.
When you laid your hands on me
I went to tell, put in a jail cell.
Your rules weren't in the certificate.
I've never been married before,
Now I'm kicked.
I did all you said
and I admit I'm a handful,
but now you're the fool.
You broke promises to our children and to me
Now it's you I no longer want to see.
Your jealousy is overwhelming.
You don't care about yourself.
Behind closed doors I now am afraid.
Good luck as you're by yourself.

Blamed

I was only a child.
I don't know what age.
The three of us played.

We were babysat.
I started to be bad.
The end is so sad.

One of us had a special gift.
An extra chromosome to live with.

She never was smacked before,
till the night I started the storm.

She was out of control,
so for the first time she got a scold.

He woke in the night later and told
his love, "I shouldn't have scolded."

He never woke again.
He died of a heart attack.
I was blamed, for he was never to come back.

If I'd just behaved that night,
things wouldn't be the same.
From child till now,
I'm still the one to blame.

It's such a shame.
I gave my son his name.

Blind

Can I see with my eyes open?
I've lost my own devotions.
Bewildered, circled everywhere.
People say I don't care.
He's got my soul; he's got my feet.
I know I have to defeat.
the peace, the truth, the living.
My life needs a shift.
One, two, three, gone—
yet because of Jesus I still go on.
Still is a fright.
I still smile, but I run.
I no longer can see.
I no longer know me.
Up and down success.
Now I can't see at all.
Drugs and alcohol found me,
when I wished for death on me,
as a child till now, to keep.
My will keeps failing somehow.
Why, oh, why won't you help me?
I continue not to see reality.
The truth hurts, so much guilt and shame.
The Lord come and came.
The Lord wants me to see,
but I continue to be blind.
Afraid to jump, to stop the pain.
Lord, I can't stay blind.

Born

Our first love,
as she came out of my womb.
Your life just changed, so soon.

Our eyes met first, as if she knew,
what you went through.

Tears in all faces,
so much love exchanged.

The most beautiful innocence to see,
after coming out of mommy.

Right away you hold her little hands,
greeting her to the skies, to the land.
There's no other moment shared between me and you, honey.
We just combined each other's love to create our beautiful baby

Bounce

Thoughts of moving linger,
for him or her.
Would you risk what you got
just because for that instant you forgot?
Moments come and go.
Don't let certain things in life show.
Vows are sacred to God.
Don't give up what you got.
Love is only once.
Don't let the ball bounce.

Caged

I started out lost,
and I'm still paying the cost.

I do not know who I am,
or whom I'm supposed to be.
Too many doors to unlock,
I can't find the keys.

Dramatic episodes
from child till now,
yet I'm still alive somehow.

People say I can find myself,
even though I've run my whole life.
I never fit in;
I've been caged all my life.

When recovery starts you start in age where you started at.
Who knew the first time I used,
not realizing I was in self abuse.

The cage is nothing but all the shame.
You'll never be the same.
You no longer have your identity.
When, unlocked, you're still in pain.

You either learned your lesson or not,
if you pick up right away 'cause you forget
what you were punished for.
Then you lose your keys to the door.

So after enough punishment you raised.
The forgiveness has been given so you can stay out of the cage.

Cleansed

I cleansed myself in prayers at four A.M. within.
I couldn't sleep from severe nightmares
of where I am and could have been.

Consequences now scare me,
for they never did accept regret.
I have to cleanse myself in prayers to be forgiven and forget.

I can't forget the lessons that won't be learned.
I wish I had holy water in my shower to cleanse the burns.

The roses in bloom didn't bring the love, except for myself pleasures.
The spells are false. The spirits is measured, cleanse me,
for my sins still continue.

Does my myth cleanse me? How to cleanse
even the sin I don't remember, so the water washes the sins to You.

Christmas Snow

I woke up in the morning with the smell of crisp of snow.
I believe I was the first to know.

The snow reflections stuck to my window.
The diamonds show.

You snuggle up to your best so fast,
not even caring about breakfast.

Dreaming all just white.
Can't wait to have a snowball fight.

Build your own imagination of a snowman,
before you again see land.

Wouldn't want this to be on Jesus' day.
The most perfect way every Christmas day.

Clouds

First as I lie on the grounds and stare,
as the shapes change in the air,

first I see an elephant.
Now I see a dragon.
Next I see a talking penguin.

The car drives slow,
with the movement of snow.

The sword looks scary.
The unicorn is such a beauty.

The puppy is barking,
then he flies closer to me.

The eagle looks mean.
The dolphin is swimming.

I could look and use my imagination all day.
What do your clouds say?

Crooked

Was I born crooked?
What has God forgot in me?
Was I under a rock
when God created the university?

People avoid us in every way,
alone again today.

Amongst my own mind
where the sun don't shine.

A crooked life, unexplained.
Nobody is the same.

The invisible tattoo carries out
trouble, love, and pain to make you shout.

Some days I'm perfect, others too insane to be me.
Chemistry changes constantly.

We cry ourselves to sleep.
This disease we don't want to keep.

The gift can be a gift.
We always over give.

Hidden talents, only we know.
If you're afraid, normal will never be your own.

Stop being crooked; everyone has a special gift.
Jesus will give you a lift.

Crutch

I miss you so much,
your love and touch.
I need my crutch.

Your scent your breath.
Now I can't feel it when you breathe.
It's just you I need to see.

Why are you so far away,
making a difference of our Independence Day?

You are my heart and my soul.
Without you I've let my emotions go.

Now I'm only numb.
Being without you is no fun.

I worry more and more every day.
I breathe in so much, I no longer can say.

I need you here with me.
Without my crutches, I'm a catastrophe.

I need you
to get me through.

My friends tell me not to use you as a crutch,
although I love you so much.

I know I'll see you in time.
My friends are keeping me alive.

When alone my mind goes within.
That's when I start breathing anything in.
Oh God, please help me,

Decision

or my love I'll never again see.
Your time has come,
never a chosen date.
Another decision to be made,
false to your fate.

The Lord looks at you with peace,
with complete acceptance.
We all have different circumstances.

Mankind verses Mother Nature.
We always think we have another turn.
None of us want to burn.

The answer is always in front of you.
Sometimes you just can't let go.
Angels are there
and the Holy Ghost too.

You think of your loved ones
and the helpless ones.
You want part ownership individually,
the ups and downs to save it all alone?

So you choose the Holy Ghost
Or you'll never be properly seen.
The Devil creates bad dreams.

Are you giving up true desires to do the right thing?
I know sometimes it's hard to see.

Just give your first waking breath to the Lord
and make the right decisions as the Earth still turns.
Keep up your spirits, so you make the right turn.

Desperate

I've wished and prayed,
but I gave up too fast.
The longer I wait,
the stronger the past.

Changes can be done;
can you blame me for not knowing?
There's a least one breath a day
when I want to throw in the towel.

To drop to the bottom
and never be awake.
How do I solve this
with so many mistakes.

One is too many
when it all connects.
I'm tired of staying; I'm too scared.
I'm not ready yet.

Jesus, if You hear me, please?
I'm doing all this at last.
Lift the cravings
and help me to deal with the past!

Put me where I belong
and change me,
to Our purpose of life, to
things I never handled or seen.

So much time
has been wasted,
Yet I'm so close
I can almost taste it.

Out of fear of normal,
something I never achieved,
no more dreaming,
I'm praying on my hands and knees,

desperately.

Diseased

I still remember his voice saying
"I don't want to come home and find you in the kitchen dead!"
"One more huff and you'll have no head!"

I still huffed again.
I lost my boyfriend.

I lost all my friends.
Did I think people wouldn't let go till the end?

I still hear his voice in tears.
Losing what I wanted for years.

We promised sobriety.
I never made it clean.

I still hear his voice when I huff.
Now I'm in fear of each huff.

So I tried to huff him away.
So I could let go of the pain.

Each huff became worse.
Now I'm cursed

This fucking disease won't go away.
I wish I never huffed the first day.

Now I can't even say.
I don't huff today.

I still know this is a disease,
Will I hear you till my dying day?

Now put-down flashbacks still haunt me.

Disguise

I'm sorry I have a disease!
You looked in my eyes,
with a disguise.
Who knew you were capable?
Who knew you were able?

Crossing the line.
Where were the signs?
The unexpected turn, and
all you wanted for me was to burn.

It seemed we were so close.
Now I hate that I know.
Why me?
Do you do this to everyone?
Did you perfectly seek
to make me weak?

Was this to make you feel strong?
So I couldn't go on?

Well, you made a mistake.
A chance you did not take,

to get to know me.
One thing you'll never see.

You created real emotion.
Do you know devotion?

Will you ever know?
People like you just go

in and out of a disguised life.
You are the knife.
All your stabs will leave you alone for the rest of your life.

Don't Doubt

I always think about you
in every loving way.
No matter what you need,
I'll be there every day.

I wish you wouldn't doubt me
when I need you so much.
I wish you would trust me,
even when things are tough.

I sacrifice so much for you.
I live every second for you.

Your every moment ticks from
your sweet heart.
I'll never let you go,
or do anything wrong when were apart.

Making love to you is everything.
It's all in our rings.
Don't you know by now, I just don't do anything?

I love you so much.
It's me you have to trust.
For me to be with you,
it's a must!

You are my only honey.
You'll always be the other half of me.
Don't doubt my love which is true.
I just want it to be just you and me.

Everyone

We've all been through a process,
whether we admit it or not.
To overcome it
is an understanding, or a plot.

Everyone wants to help.
Everyone has an answer.
How can you really help me
if there is a cure for him or her?

Everyone is different,
Yet everyone is the same.
Circumstances of past lives
hopefully teach us how to plan the game.

One will tell the message.
We decide whether to give or receive.
Sometimes we listen,
but who to take the unknown need?

Education is taught.
Experience is not the same.
Everyone knows,
decisions will always remain.

Family

I will be the best lover,
and mom I could be.
Share with you, only in trust.
I'll try to be all I can be.

We don't forget to pray as one,
to the One who is responsible for
all He's done.

We'll thank Him every day when we wake;
nothing the Devil can't take.

To finally get what we deserve,
for the life, love, serenity, peace, and respect.
Earning what the Heavens wish the best.

To guide us, teach us, and
to learn from our mistakes.
That we grow together
and protect our new family.

I thank Him for you every day,
thanking him for my husband and our children.
As long as He rules our lives
and we keep praying.

Let's thank the Lord in every way we can.
I never thought I'd ever give up and vow.
If you never came,
I wouldn't have made it to now.

Flying

Why can't I fly away?
God and I can't handle the pain.
I prayed, I cried, and I threatened my life.
Things are too tight.
Why do I have to cry.
Why can't you help me?
I can't see.
I would take care of anyone, but no one takes care of me.
The love I crave—
I'm too weak.
How hard are you testing me?
If this proceeds,
I'll tell you the truth.
Could I fly off the highest roof?
My tears are real,
and I'm landing down,
but the world keeps going around.
When will my wings heal?
Why isn't it real?
I'm begging again.
As I reach for your hands.

Free?

Free as a bird.
Freedom to drive.
Free as love.
Freedom to arrive.

Tried to fly.
Unable to drive.
Tried to love.
Unable to freely survive.

Freeze

What would you do
the second everything freezes?
The end of the world.
Not even a breeze.

Where will you be in your soul
when it's time to go?

Frozen in our sins.
Where have you been?

It's not our choice anymore.
To Heaven or Hell, are you sure?

Was your faith with God
enough to save you?
Did you give up and
just hope you'd make it through?

Gentlemen's Day Care Center

First you have to look your best.
You come to work decent.
You leave home the rest.
Disguise yourself as an entertainer,
so no one outside the doors recognizes her.
You put on your special show
and just let yourself go.
Put on a smile and
shake what your mama gave you.
And then you'll make more mucho.
Change your outfit, all different and unique.
Find the customer.
That's your key.
Make eye contact with him or her, and be polite.
And dance your ass off all night.
Treat all your men like gold,
young or old.
Pick songs to the mood,
and make the right moves.
Stick to the rules, don't take a chance.
Or you'll have to find somewhere else to dance.
Don't be jealous or start a fight,
or you'll be gone for a while, poor and not right.
Keep your tempo on the pole.
Don't get drunk or drugged.
Everyone will know!
Present yourself with respect and pride.
Do not cry!
Don't share problems of your own.
If they wanted that, they would have stayed home.
Every man has his own type.
Don't worry, you'll have your night.
As long as you take excellent care of yourself,
and smile even if you're not in the mood,
The G-Spot will be the bar for you.

Grandad

Granddad, you always took my side.
Now I can't hide.
You're up so high.
I can feel your presence in the sky.

Granddad, you've always took my tears,
through all the years.
You ease the pain.
Not having you here is not the same.

Granddad, I'll never believe you left me
even as you rose.
The love remains
as you made it home.

Granddad, my tears fall for you,
Don't worry, I can get through.
I look up to you.
I thank God for you.

Granddad, I would like to pray to you.
I don't know what I'd do,
if it hadn't been for you.
I wouldn't or could not know what to do.
I'll always love you.

Granddad, you always went out of your way.
Your love for your family stays.
Be with your wife too.
She misses you.
I'll be there for her for you.

Granddad, I still cry.
I never got the chance to say goodbye.
Please never leave my side.
I wish you didn't die.

Grandmoms

All grandmothers are so sweet.
They always have a special treat.

From our birth till after death.
They count our every breath.

Rocking us in a rocking chair while
singing to you and reading and telling stories too.

Guiding our every step as we grow
and telling us things we need to know.

Cooking and cleaning for family tides,
taking in all family sides.

Keeping all relatives together the best they can.
Cards and gifts always sent.

Grandmas are the best in the world.
I can't wait till it's my turn!

Halloween

Scary costumes, monsters, and super heroes,
dressing up to their creations and
hanging up scary decorations.

Trick or treat around the towns.
Walking the streets disguised, up and down.

Who is who? How much candy will I get?
No curfews, I'm not done yet.

Sometimes a trick to fright you,
that will always remain with you.

Scary movies, carved lit pumpkins, and
money or candy for the hungry munchkins.

The night finally silent in its own scare.
Nobody, nowhere.

The parents are not checking all your candy for safety.
Happy Halloween!

Boo!

Hold onto the Sky

Everyone loses hope some days.
Don't let the Devil get in your way.
Heaven is waiting for you,
so do the best you can do.
Hope is what keeps the sky alive.
Faith is for the better life.
Sometimes it might rain and pour
and you just want to cower away.
It's the tests of life, to see if
you can look at Jesus eye to eye,
to accept the truth of whom we really are.
Souls can go so far.
Live each day like it is your last.
Don't live in the past.
Life on earth is too fast.
Hold on to the sky no matter what
occurs in your mind.
I know the world can seem so unkind.
Hold on to the sky,
as it holds on to your life.

How Do I?

How do I explain my love to you?
How do I make you believe it's true?

The first time we ever met,
you were there for me. I'll never forget.

I waited for you at a hotel.
When you didn't show I couldn't tell.

I was on my way to work and I knew I was falling for you,
even though I waited alone, the whole night through.
I wrote my thoughts to you.

I hope you were surprised when I first kissed you,
and later we made love and I know you loved me too.

If we only knew then what we know now,
this accident wouldn't have happened somehow.

Now I can't even think of touching you.
We both cheated on our son.
We tried again to be,
but the cheating wasn't done.

You left the state with our son.
How do I pick what state to be?
I have two teens in New Jersey.

You left your first kids when we all could have been together.
Forgiveness, never!

Don't think this is so over because
you gave him up so you can move on!
I'm coming to be his mom!

Hungry

I wake you almost every night.
Hungry with my...tight.

You're tired at first, but then I go...
Then I lick you and all around.

I kiss your lips and say I love you.
Are you hungry? My time is due.

You start licking and...all over my spots.
Sometimes I finish and I let you watch.

Then after I climax, I climb
on top of you, ready, one, two.

It's all up inside me, up and down and
side to side
Yahoo, what a ride.

You move with me too
Till you...too.

Then,
we're hungry again.

Let the Butterflies Fly

Why can I fly,
but not with proper anonymity?
My butterfly wings were created,
for all our beauty to be seen.

Yes, I'm alive, or am I dead?
I need to develop my wings soon,
or I'll remain in a cocoon.

Instant gratification
wants me to fly now, not when.
I must give time to create my wings
or I'll fall again.

Hardly leaving the ground,
when I thought I was flying high.
Numbness prevented
all flights.

I forget the stages
of metamorphosis.
One day at a time,
or the other butterflies I'll miss.

I must pray for patience.
Life will always fly by,
and I know I can make a butterfly fly.

Now it's my turn to bloom
Why did I waste my time
when Jesus wants all His butterflies to fly.

Loving

Loving, staring, hoping, charming, caring,
holding, kissing, hugging, cuddling,
understanding, sharing, playing, daring,
giving, dancing, singing, writing, reading,
abiding, committing, opening, laughing, crying,
hearing, helping, securing, intertwining,
trusting, praying, marrying, baring, loving.

Met

The toughest part is the introduction,
when the conversations
always end in agony
of the most broken hearted.

The sieve, the size of love, can rupture
or begin at any time.
What do we know?
Love is blind.

When two are connected
and a third steps in.
Living your lie
shall not be seeing within.

If you're not truly happy,
then why put yourself through it?
Then you remember,
when it's too late for this.

Both met other hearts,
now broken in two.
There's only one thing I know is true.

The one you never cheat on,
for all your lives—
Then you'll be a husband, and she'll be your wife.

Midnight

It's the time of the year,
when the last sixty seconds we come together as one.
The stroke of midnight brings cheer.

Parties of life everywhere.
Family and friends all share.

Toasts of glasses join together.
Another year passes forever.

That moment of special words
and kisses, hugs, and fireworks.

Midnight is everyone's turn.
The feeling of being reborn.

To start over again into the continuing years.
HAPPY NEW YEAR!

Mirrors

How could we be blind to see?
The reflections were cracked endlessly.
Now the image is so clear.
He's so sweet and dear.

He can make the unseen laugh.
He can accomplish any task.
His words will comfort you.
He sees beauty in the sun and the moon.

He sticks to his own attire.
He's soft as a feather and
his passion is a fire.

He brings out the best of himself.
Loving him is like a spell.
The softness of his eyes makes you fall.
It's amazing what he went through, he can love at all.

He stopped and met me
and realized the mirror can see.
Real love was never found
until he found the reflections of me.

Then he said something before he couldn't see.
That true love was none, until he looked at me.
Now the mirror has become one.
The cracks of bad luck are gone.

Not only do you see me.
You're the only reflection I see.

Mommy Dearest

Mommy dearest, I couldn't tell you, what I was going through.

No choice of food.
No choice where to live.
Mommy dearest, I couldn't let you give.

I already had so much pain as you raised me.
I just wanted to be independent
and proud.
I was silent to you for respect,
yet my mind was so loud.

Problems I can't solve.
Problems always resolved.
Mommy dearest, it wasn't your fault.

Mommy dearest, you raised me right.
I always loved you through.
My problems, I'll keep to myself.
If you were the same, I know I'd help you.

Misunderstood

The integrity is not misconcepted.
Hardly ever accepted.

Our mind is confusing us.
Doctor's make a fuss.

We don't want others to see.
Is it our fault for our disabilities?

We try to pretend to be normal,
but those voices and visions are unexpectedly informal.

Music isn't loud enough all the time.
Silence is made with each tick of time.

The biggest exam is in within us in all.
It's worse when peer pressure calls.

Replacement always fails.
Misunderstood, institutions, death, or jail.

Can there be foundations to correct us.
Whether we're down or up?

We're more creative than others.
Better senses mixed all together.

Observant yet stupid things done to ourselves, and lovingly kind.
I had to control mine.

Substances only make us more understood.
We'd have control if we could.

I'm tired of being understood.
Treat us the way you should!

Money Spell

In the vigilance of my thoughts
I got caught. My purpose had to be sought.
As the blessing smoked the room,
hoping money would come soon.
This spell I had to send,
so I could lend,
people in need.
I lit it to proceed.
The very next day money came our way.
Not in greed, but for people in need.
Only to loved ones and friends,
where love and friendship don't end.
I lift this spell for all of you.
Let the spell see us through.

My Angel

My Angel will always grow
as I grow with my mistakes.
What I breathe in
has it takes.
My respect, my running away, and my pride,
my Lord keeps me alive.
As the wings flutter and speak to me, as I see,
I fall to my knees.
Peace during Earth has a hard touch.
I've been through too much.
I wouldn't still be here today, and my prayers aren't answered right away.
I only get what Heaven deserves.
I can't run anywhere anymore.
So I'll run with my angel,
so I can fly to Heaven's door. I thank my angel for staying with me.
anytime I'm in need.

My Teddy Bear

My teddy bear is as cute as can be.
As I cuddle him, he cuddles me.

So tender, so soft,
he goes everywhere with me so he won't get lost.

He's purple and his name is Teddy.
Anytime I need love, he is ready.

Sometimes I awaken from my loft and he's on the floor.
It's like I knew in my sleep to awaken.
I pick him up immediately and make sure he's okay,
then off to dreaming as we're both sleeping.

He's the best bear in the world,
except the one who is human.
That is the one who won him for me,
my husband.

So I have two teddy bears dear to me.
My wonderful husband and Teddy.

Near

The end of time is near.
Revelations is here.
The sun is dissolving every day.
The ozone layer has nowhere to lay.
Pollution chokes the world.
The world is starting to burn.
The asteroid unannounced to our birth,
heading directly to earth.
Addictions creating suicides,
or born sick for life.
Not enough pills to find cures.
The plants are no longer pure.
The flood arises so high from the all the seas.
You no longer can breathe.
War and destruction mess up their minds.
The near is no longer blind.
It's almost our time.

Neglected

Have I neglected my life?
Always grabbing the knife?
I was always giving up to soon,
so impatient to again use.
Not having my priorities straight,
still being afraid
to live a normal life, as I was
so use to flying like a kite.
Neglecting other's needs and
just thinking of how to run from me,
not realizing who I hurt.
Taking the chances of being burnt.
Now people don't take me as a priority,
because I neglected me.
How do I take all my mistakes back?
Instead I'm still getting attacked.
No one seems to understand.
I was so abused, I did all I can.
Now I let go of the past,
but no matter what I finish last.

Once Upon a Dream

All that desired pain is free?
I was insane.
I did not ask to live this way.
We all learn something every day.

Hopes and dreams destroyed,
from something unknown.
We never quite say no.

Don't you lie? It's all inside.
We all will face it when we die.
Truth is harder than running.
You're the only enemy where you're heading.

Crept inside, awake or asleep,
the sun will rise again to awake, once upon a dream.

Pool

It's finally my turn to rack, as I put the balls in order, nice and tight.
Your opponent getting ready to break, with the pool stick stoking right.

The balls break and scatter against the felt.
Sometimes one or two go in,
or it remains open for you to pick yourself.

You look over the table,
to decide if you want solid or stripes.
Like a chess board you choose.
You hit the ball in,
now it's the beginning of the fight.

You take turns, shooting them in one by one.
Are you serious, or just playing for fun?

Now shooting your best,
trying to get as many in.
I play defense,
so you, opponent, can't get an easy shot in.

Back and forth you play,
going to the end, with the eight.
Hardly any balls on the table,
Now you have to calmly concentrate.

Will I hit in the eight.
No winner till the fat lady sings.
Playing till I hopefully win.
Killing the King.

The crowd watches till the end
for their time to play.
Cutting the grass, taking the dog for a walk, kisses, cuts, geometry,
combinations, and easy shots, but don't leave it for them to have a way.

Now at the end, it is time.
The next gets ready to play,
as the eight ball sinks in.
Who's next to play me? I say.

Progressed

She says it plays over and over again.
Every laugh, hit, touch, and word,
yet you never held her.

Your only job was selling drugs.
She said you hardly got a shower.
When she waited for you,
she waited for hours.

Drugs always came first,
and that's what you fed her too.
They killed each other and
could have killed her embryo too.

You were not even her race,
which was her first.
You took advantage of her loneliness and sadness
and made love burst.

Desperate to leave her memories again,
now further in her heart,
now she and her son are apart.

Why did this happen?
Addictions progressed, you see.
When they took her son away,
she had you locked up without a key.

They still remain friends after sobriety now.
The lessons were taught somehow,
except he is free
while you remain without raising your own baby.

How can she forgive you after she said no so many times?
She said it was like candy. She couldn't stop eating.

How are you kind?

You're different people now, but it's too late.
She can rest without you, but can't sleep without her baby!

Promised

I have no one to dream tonight.
I have no one to hold me tight.

My tears have made me numb.
I no longer trust in fun.

Where were you when I needed you?
I waited all day.
Now there's nothing you can say.
I needed you most today.

My heart has ached so many times, depending on you.
Did I promise too?

Chasing that one scene
of the past of you and me.

Am I being punished for something?
Wasted time promising?

Now I sit here all alone.
No visits, no phone.
What did you do wrong?

Well, single again now.
No promises for you,
and I'll tell all others not to accept any promises from you.

Punishment

Why am I being punished?
Why am I so impatient?

Why am I so stubborn?
Why was I born?

Why can't I sing?
Why can't I have my dreams?

Why can't I help all?
Why can't I get over this wall?

Why am I constantly used?
Why have I been constantly abused?

Why can't I stay clean?
Why can I be so mean?

Why do I cheat?
Why do people trigger me?
Why do I screw up my destiny?

Why won't the Devil leave me alone?
Why won't the friends pick up the phone?

Why can't I keep a job?
Why does my pain throb?

Why do I still ask why?
Will I be punished for asking why?

Push

Why did you push me?
I thought you loved me.

Just because I wanted to do my own things,
you would start fighting.

Why do I push you to all your limits?
Am I pushing all your buttons,
till someone calls the cops in?

We've yelled, pushed, punched, broken and thrown things.
Who pushes more, you or me?

I'm sick what's your excuse?
I know I'm not being used.

We've been through Hell's circumstances.
Can we fix this?
From tempers to substances.

I love you.
Can we get through this too?

If you push me again, in any way,
I might not come back some day.

Rescue Me

Rescue me from my loneliness and pain.
I cannot remain the same.

Days and nights combine as one,
As I lay I get nothing done.

My choices are caught
like nothing has been taught.

My tears make me sick.
Old habits are mostly kicked.

Now I have no rewards.
Struggling with swords, still all alone.
Need hope,
so hard on my own.

My life has fallen before my eyes.
There is no disguise.

Please help, I'm going down.
I feel I'm already underground.

Rescue me now with love and faith. Rescue my past's pain.
Love is what I need and then I will rescue you the same.

Rewind

If I could rewind time, you wouldn't have caught me.
Never any handcuffs and not embarrassed by suicide.

If I could rewind time, things I couldn't say.
If I did you'd remember till your dying day.

If I could rewind time I would have said I loved you.
Never now will these dreams be true—will I ever see you?

If I could rewind time, I wouldn't have taken it out on you
Now you're alone too.

If I could rewind time, you still would be here with me,
but now I'm still angry, for I took the blame from you to me.

See

You don't think I can see.
I'm smarter then you.
You're going the wrong way.
Soon there won't be any more of us two.

You call every second.
You're up my ass.
I'm accused of flirting
even if someone just passes.

What the fuck is wrong with you?
I married you!

You broke every promise.
I'm trying to be understanding of your past.
Now it keeps happening.
How long will this last?

It is starting to hurt me.
Can't you see?

See me!
If you don't get help,
I can't continue.
Soon it will be just you.

Someone else will see and won't doubt or threaten me.
I love you, but it's too bad it's me you'll never see.

Sneaky

I was sneaky as long as I can remember,
from January to December.

I'll be behind you and you won't know.
As you jump, that's my show.

I'll knock you out so I can go out,
Praying you're still asleep when I sneak in my ways.

Things I stole
were the best things for free.
I'm so quick, you don't see me.

Look at you straight in the eyes
and tell you lies.
I had a good time.

When I know you're not looking or unaware,
don't be surprised.
I'm a sneak when you least realize.

I can't break this habit,
for I had do it to survive.
If I said I'm not a sneak,
I lied.

Shining Faces

My love can shine,
if you want to see.
The others that glow
will be the only ones to see.

Others are afraid of the glare,
trying to break the shells every day.
Sometimes I try to help.
They go on their own way.

Just as I would be,
if the Devil stole my moment,
by ignoring Jesus
and all the messages He sends me.

So do I mock you or try to help?
Do I run from you?
Which way do I go?
You creep up on me everywhere.
Which is easier to know?

The shining faces,
I need twenty-four hours a day,
because when I'm alone, I'll try to do it my way.

I wish Jesus could protect me from all.
My heart wounds make me ill.
Now my shield grew,
in the falls of will.

The harder I fight,
the brighter the shine.
Slowly come the changes
and new ways to survive.

I pray for all the shining faces to stay near me.
I cannot forget,
if I lose the shining faces,
I will create regrets.

Subject Eyes

Pronouncing our charm,
in different ways.
Hiding the talent and
lost in what our eyes say.

Changes of life.
Too many seasons.
Dreams now in doubt for
too many reasons.

We searched our hearts.
Who is played?
It all comes together
after the Lord trains.

The butterflies smile,
twinkling in our sleep.
High in the dreamy skies,
but for keeps?

Enough broken hearts,
desperation is near
to self-destruction,
to obscene fears.

Now what do we do?
Is love an option or gone?
Falsely accused,
how do we move on?

Then suddenly those subject eyes beauties arrive again.
The long nights have come to the end.
Clashes seem impossible
So we both pray.
Is this making believe?

Is lovely finally here to stay?

We know right and wrong, chance could be a dare.
When it comes to you, all I can do is stare.

Now no broken hearts and no tears in our eyes.
I knew from the start, those eyes would become mine!

Sweet Winds

Let me feel Your sweet winds as they pass me by. I float like feathers as
I start to cry.

'Cause the truth shall set me free, and You're so sweet to come along
and sweep me off my feet.

At times of troubles and pain, You always took the blame.

So now I would like to thank You for this new air I breathe
any time that I am in need.

And if I see someone in trouble too,
I'll give them a breath and send them up to You.

Survivor

I've fallen in so many places.
I've seen so many faces.

The Lord is still there,
through the triumphs and despair.

Sometimes I feel like giving up.
Putting knives to my throat.
Each time it's a different hurt.

I always thought I was a…because I couldn't do.
Now I don't want the Devil to have my soul.
I know there are other you's.
We can't just let it go.

Addictions are a slow death.
If we don't stop, we'll always regret.

Our love will disappear if we
keep running away.
We want to do things our own way.

A survivor I have become,
because the Devil doesn't deserve us.
Even before you open your eyes,
give it to Jesus.

We all are survivors
for a reason,
So let's stop cheating.

Try your best to follow His commandments.
It may hurt at first.
Jesus picked us to survive;
He's the main source of our thirst.

The Crow

The skids on our knees,
the drowning of the soul,
as we go on, we create more holes.
Black is our death.
We all try to get away.
Now we have become the prey.
They wander right through you.
There's nowhere to hide.
As they start pecking,
we start to fly.
The blood drips on your eyes.
You no longer can see.
They pick even more
to kill the key.
The blood drips on.
We start missing.
Then they steal your brain and seal it with kisses.
Now you're blind.
Nothing to see.
Now I'm another crow to see.
Now the drowning is over for another.
Now who will suffer too?
Now that he drowned me,
I'll fly after you.

The Hawk

The hawks feed off the dead,
the one thing most dread.
Preying on once-living souls
just so they can grow.
So what do we know as we grow?
Are you afraid of your own soul?
Do you know where you'll go?
What do we do to grow
without eating other souls?
He does not want us to be a hawk
that feeds off the dead.
He doesn't want us to dread to be dead.
Death, when it comes your time,
living you were given all the signs.
Watch where you fly in life.
Follow the faith in God's eyes.
You don't want the devil to have his doom.
Don't do what a hawk can and will do.

The Lucky Pen

When you have a lucky pen,
you'll know when.
The ink will flow.
The words will let go.
Mine blinks in different colors,
yellow, orange, green, purple and blue.
Some people have pens not just to write
but to draw too.
If you're lucky enough to have a lucky pen,
you'll never want to let go of it till the end.

The Night

Let's save the night,
in the dark, in the fright.
You cannot see.
What's around me?
I hear this, I hear that.
Did I just feel something touch my back?
The only relief is the twinkles in the sky.
Will God get you by?
Unexpected in every way.
like in a scare of a hole.
No hand to hold.
No one can hear you.
You don't know what to do
to save the night till dawn,
or can't you hold on?

The Rings

The rings of life cannot hide.
They connect it all.
No more withdrawals.

I'll help you with what I've been through,
and then I'll help you grow through the show.

But I need you all to sing to bring
the peace to me, from sea to see,

to the clouds above,
the stars with love,

till the night wraps the wrongs,
to end with the beauty of the dawns.

To let you know, we'll always grow.

For the purpose of love,
Our purposes are from above.

The rings of life continue on
in the beauty of all minds
of our songs,
where we combine.
Let's all sing along.

The Spell

First I'll cast my blood on the stone.
The drips that only the Devil and me will grow.

I kissed the envelope with the access blood
only with hope of love.

The letter was opened, with no clue to you.
I cast a spell on you.

I kissed the stone every night,
hoping my dreams dawn on you tonight.

As I wait, the dream never comes true.
I already know that I love you.

Ten times a curse came upon.
Instead he met someone else and moved on.

Love has to be real and true,
but I sure would have loved for that spell to work
on us, to make you love me too.

The Walk

Jesus is taking me for a walk,
for I could not see.
He showed me my sins
and helped me find me.

I have fought with all my power
to do it my way.
Now I'm locked up
for the price I have to pay.

Most of my problems
started with drug and alcohol abuse.
If I ever had a wish,
I'd wish I never used.

How can I be so insane?
After sitting here all this time,
I'm still craving crack cocaine.

Don't get me wrong.
I want my friends and family, not drugs too.
I never realized
that each time I used, I was hurting You, you, and you.

I was committing suicide the slow way.
All alone I thought, till I walked with Jesus that day.

Now at my first waking breath I get on my knees,
Thanking Jesus for walking me through.

Tides

Tides brought from the moon.
Isn't that amazing?
How long will the sun remain blazing.
Photosynthesis is not the same.
The Earth is losing its flames.
Yet growing pollution,
smoke from revolutions.
I'm surprised the blue sky
we still can see, as we thrive.
Can the whole world
be controlled by mankind,
or does Mother Nature danger the tides?

Tongues

I talked to You
in our own language,
and I fell to the ground.
Satan got so pissed, He threw me down.

He wants to know what I'm praying to You.
He's trying to break our faith,
because during our conversations, He can't get through.

It's always easier to sin than to serve.
I know what we deserve.

I will pray in tongues more and more,
so only You can hear me.

Will the Devil become angered more and more with me?
What's the next trick up His sleeve?

I've sinned so much, even today.
I always ask for forgiveness, every second I pray.

Please, Lord, keep the Devil away from me!
So we can help all love in peace, eternally.

You're the only One
who can save me by my prayers in tongues!

To the Heavens

Each breath to the top,
Eager to see
Heaven's beauty.

Thoughts going through my mind
to make it to the next step,
a spiral of circles to hope, but I wasn't there yet.

As I reached the top,
relief came through me.
I couldn't believe all the beauty.

The sun at the horizon and the
clouds lit on the outside.
Purple and orange skies all around,
with the Lord close to my side.

The seagulls flying free, and
the ocean waves splashing the stones.
I still breathed,
but I knew I was close to home.

The breezes uplifted me, blowing through my hair.
I felt peace surrounding me everywhere.
This I had to share.

Your thoughts of imagination wander in the air,
things to have you arouse.
After all of this, you won't want to
leave the top of the lighthouse.

Tourist

I was a tourist
of the other side of the Hoover Dam.
At that time I had a man.

We received a course and put our life jackets on.
Then as we paddled, the boat moved beyond.

Looking at the rocks that looked as if they were going to fall.
The trees were the colors of fall, so many, so tall.

Listening to the water wallow
where the water is deep and shallow.

We took snack breaks and pulled to the side.
We wandered off to hide.

The birds everywhere,
fish jumping up and down.
As a tourist I took pictures all around.

Now the tour is over, the peace
will stay with you for a while.

I will not be a tourist at that same location from below.
I've christened the place with love.
One of the tourist sights made from above.
Where's the next place we'll go?

Trees

There are trees in my life
that grew with my time.

All have different meanings,
all in different scenery.

The first time I remember, I wasn't allowed to climb,
at my little grandmom's yard.
I'd climb as high as I could go,
taking the dare without a guard.

I grew a tree from school.
It grew with nourishment with me from the ground.
I was so hurt when my ex-stepdad chopped it down.

Another tree for all, a surprise each year,
a gathering together of families.
Always a different Christmas tree.
I'll never forget when my mother saw mine and said,
"Your tree you decorated better than me."
I told her, "I learned from you, Mommy."

Away from the city a tree stood all alone in the middle of nowhere.
I was scared like poltergeist, yet curious.
Later the lightning struck right there.

I climbed another kind of tree,
but this time I got stuck in one.
I just couldn't jump as all made fun.
After I finally made it down from the tree,
I hurt one person who should have helped me.

The last tree still remains in National Park, NJ.
After my mother's death, I engraved her name, "MOM."
It's still her as her spirit goes on.
I know this because her plot I find with a tree, a part of her and me.

These trees all carry so much,
the challenges within me.
Emotion, love, fears, happiness, daring, and tears.

Now the question for the you in me,
What was your favorite tree?

Truth

Don't come around me!
Disappeared dreams is all I see.

I'll just stay here alone,
Yet I'll always be known.

Wait to see what I write next,
published in a text.

I'm not myself, trustworthy,
for the life I've seen.

I keep asking what to do.
Stubborn continues when the answer is true.

I can preach the truth so bluntly,
yet I burnt all my bridges
from loved ones and family.

Convincing strength has all been there.
My instincts brought me nowhere.

A scary life I have preceded.
I'm even afraid of me.

Running away from the truth, I no longer can lie.
Now my truth will be in your eyes.

Tunes

I awaken with a tune in my head every day.
A different song each day.
Boy, I hope I hear it today.

The alarm goes off with music of a different song.
I listen with a snooze, too tired to sing along.

It keeps the voices in my head busy.
Music twenty-four seven.
I sing, dancing to the beat,
dancing feet to seat.

I never thought I had to be scared of the songs
that play in silence some nights and days.

I feel the voices pick the tune to play.

Waiting

I've waited so long to achieve my dreams.
Opportunities never seen.

I'm forty-one now and still waiting. What did I do wrong,
since a child still panting.

I poured with all my heart and soul.
I let every thought and let the pen flow.

Blunt, talented, creative, imaginative, and smart.
Thinking when will I also create dreams apart.

I've been writing since I had a crayon in my hand.
Hoping to have world fans.

Growing to help someone,
in all ways, not just one.

Waiting for inspiration to go on a dream.
How much longer do I have to wait on me?

I want to turn heads and expand
imaginations and opinions of your own.
Waiting makes me feel alone.

Where?

Although it's been so long since you've been in my life,
I shouldn't still cry.

I know as a child, I never fit in anywhere,
but I know at first, you treated me fair.

I know I did a lot of bad things in your eyes.
After my abuse, I had to do what I had to do to survive.

I do remember all the good and bad times.
I'm sharing it in your rhyme.

I remember when you and mom were together a
nd when you were apart for good.
I still don't understand why or what should.

I'll tell you the love I remember, the love we once had.
Don't you remember when we were glad?

I remember the constant music, us wrestling around live on TV.
I remember all you taught me.

All the dinners, Rexy's Bar to the Pub.
While you watched football, I'd give you back rubs.

You always were there for me, correcting my wrongs,
pointing your finger as you repeated over and over again.
I trusted you. I loved you; now we're not even friends.

Why have you left me?
Where is the love? Now it's history.

You stuck up for me when mom didn't understand.
Buying me clothes and so.
When did you let me go?

I always looked up to you, and I still try my best to obey you,
but my sister was and is your daughter too!

I'm crying right now because I don't understand.
How can I call you a father or a man?

I'm sorry I didn't listen then, but I'm listening now.
How do I get you back in my life somehow?

I'm sorry, I'm sick, an addict of anything,
bi-polar, schizophrenic, and abused.
You wonder why I used.

First I watched you and my mom beat each other up.
She constantly threw out your stuff.

After you moved on with another,
you didn't know, because of her hurt, how much we were abused at
home.
When my ex-stepdad molested me, you did nothing.
I even had an abortion from him. Did you know?

You tell people you have no kids.
Where have you been?

Dad, please forgive me. I'm not the same.
I still want you to be proud of me.
You will always be my daddy.

Please, Dad, where are you?
Wherever you are, I understand, people make mistakes. I forgive you.

Please come back. I promise I won't do wrong.
Forgive me. I need you, Dad.
I hope writing books has made you proud not sad.

Dad, I'm losing all my family, being greeted from above.
Dad, I need your love!

Before we're gone,
come back so I can write a happy poem.

Where are you?
I miss you!

Why Not Me?

She was only four years old,
living in a loving home.
Going to her home,
two seconds alone.
Missing for weeks,
then they found her sneaks in a creek.
They found her dead as they seeked.

He was about sixteen,
every girl's dream.
He had the whole team.
He went to a party one night,
and there was his fright.
Someone put something in his and his friend's drink.
They only saved one life.
Why did they want you to die?

I knew him for years.
He was always there for me.
I heard he moved out of town.
A truck hit him.
Now he's under the ground.

I went out with this kid for a while.
We were as close as we could be.
Then suddenly he dumped me.
The next girl he was with let him go.
He hung himself to let the pain go.

She was my friend but was around the block.
Consequences occur.
She had a hepatitis c
and had two twin teens.
I came over all the time.
Then one day

the new owner of the house
told me she passed away.
She never put the drugs and alcohol to her liver away.

I was about twenty-three.
I thought he would marry me.
He had to check if my cat could come too.

That was the last I heard from you.
What did you do?
Is it my fault because you were nervous for me to move in?
You picked up one time again.
They found you three days later on your floor.
I guess I'll never see you anymore.

You saved my life from the streets,
over and over again.
We became best friends
You used to smoke cigars,
then they put a tracheotomy in your throat.
I still came to see you.
I came over and they said you'd died.
All I could do was cry.

My friend since nineteen ninety-four,
me you always adored.
There for me in all ways,
till you found out that day.
CO_2 leaked from your heater.
You became weaker and weaker.
You still visited on your good days.
I think God took the wrong name.
This is insane!

Almost a brother-in-law to me,

but he drank so heavily.
He lived for a while.
He had a style.
Then things got out of hand.
Nobody gave him a helping hand.
He had nowhere to land.
One of the family members, graduation day,
he took his life away.
He wasn't invited.
So I guess he no longer could fight it.

I cut my wrists, popped pills to the extreme.
I couldn't get rid of me.
I jumped off a bridge.
I tried to drown myself.
Why not me? What does God want from me?

Without You

Being without you has me lost.
I couldn't believe the cost.

Suicide every day. Thoughts of insanity filled my ways.

You left my body, heart, and soul.
It's time to let you go.

Trying to erase all the good times.
No matter how much I try. I can't put it behind.

I kept you for years, now in all tears.

You were my best friend.
Now I can't even pretend.

Part 2: Song Lyrics

Because of You

Because of you,
I found myself again.
I want to kiss you forever,
knowing we belong together.

Because of you,
my life is so secure.
So much love,
so pure.

Because of you,
I can see the light,
and I know it feels so right.

Because of you,
I can see the light,
and I know it feels so right.

Because of you,
I learn to love.
There's nothing above you.

(Chorus)

You are the one who saved my life.
Only you stuck it out through my hard times.
I wouldn't trade you for the world.
It is the love I never heard.

BECAUSE OF YOU

Because of you,
I can smile again.
You are my best friend.

Because of you,
My tears have turned to happiness.

You brought me out of my mess.

Because of you, my heart is now open and true.
I owe it all to you.

Because of you,
I feel like a woman.
I never can wait to hold you each day again.

(Chorus)

You are the one who save my life.
You stuck it through my hard times.
I wouldn't trade you for the world.
It is a love I never heard.

BECAUSE OF YOU

My whole life has changed.
You made me beautiful
inside and out. My search is over.
My expectations are all full!

BECAUSE OF YOU

(Chorus)

You are the one who saved my life.
You stuck it out through my hard times.
I wouldn't trade you for the world.
It is the love I never heard.

BECAUSE OF YOU

BECAUSE OF YOU

B-e-c-a-u-s-e o-f y-o-u

Heartache to Heartache

Loving can be so complicated,
when it comes to me and you.
Never realizing what we had to go through.

We spoke nothing but the truth
in the beginning, especially what
we'd been through.
Never realizing it was all true.

Scared to love, scared not to.
Honey, we're not alone anymore.
The chills still remain. Never realizing
we'd grow more and more.

The past sure did disguise us.
It's a miracle we found each other.
Never realizing, we'd find one forever.

(Chorus)

Heartache to heartache,
our paths have intertwined.
Baby, please don't let the past
ruin our time.

Our touches are so real.
Our words and actions are so sweet.
Never realizing,
you swept me off my feet.

Sometimes our words change.
A flashback of old times.
Never realizing,
how far it can tear us apart.

How do we forget?
How do we forgive?
Never realizing,
our past life doesn't give.

(chorus)

Heartache to heartache,
our paths have intertwined.
Baby, please don't let the past
ruin our time.

We need to release our heads together.
Let our anger go forever.

We need to cry.
God wouldn't put us together not to try.

Baby, how can we be torn apart?
Why don't we take some time and let the happiness of us
take all the negativity?
If we don't let go of our heartaches,
there will be no more you and me.

(Chorus)

Heartache to heartache,
our paths have intertwined.
Baby, pleases don't let the past
ruin our time.

I never realized we'd be heartache to heartache as we intertwined.

Hearts Individually

The world clashes in so many ways,
changing in every way.

I say thank you and please.
I feel peace with my arms not my knees.

I'll open the door to anyone.
Hold them till their need is done.
I'll write, dance, and I sing to have fun.

I am just me
for those who want to see.

(Chorus)

Who are you?
Nobody is me.
In His eyes,
hearts are only individually.

Some have been abused.
Some have very sick ways.
They can't comprehend
why they're still here today.

Some have lost loved ones,
the closest to their hearts.
Can't pick up the pieces
or feel they have no heart.

Addicted to everything,
all ways switching one to another.
Lost all control for anything,
progressing forever.

Chemical imbalances,
pills now keep your mind right.
Overdose to narcotics with denial.
It's a constant fight.

(Chorus)
Who are you?
Nobody is me.
In His eyes,
hearts are only individually.

I have been through all of these, even lost my heart.
I want to help everyone as Jesus would.
Our hearts are individually made.
Give it all to God like we should.

Heaven Falls

(Chorus)

Well my heart will still beat.
The sun will break the dawn.
Heaven falls to lift me,
to help me carry on.

We were together so long.
I'm used to the routine.
I had no idea
that you had already left me.

As your heart beats twice now,
from one love to another.
Now I'm behind you,
as the two of you become together.

How could you pretend?
Why didn't you tell me when?
There were no differences.
How do I mend?

Now my heart is weak.
I hardly can breathe.
My memories have been dropped,
because of she.

(Chorus)

Well my heart will still beat.
The sun will break the dawn.
Heaven falls to lift me,
to help me carry on.

My trust is permanently pierced,

to never again believe.
I was so close to Heaven.
What does that mean?

I trusted in Jesus,
in His loving ways.
Heaven falls to keep you away!

If He meant for me to be betrayed,
why did you put that man in my way?

How can I trust in You,
Or was this the Devil's do?
Now all I have is You.

Tears drop from Heaven's land.
Don't want the dawn to be awakened.
It's all been taken.

(Chorus)

Well my heart still beats.
The sun still will break the dawn.
Heaven falls to lift me,
to help me carry on.

So Jesus spoke to me.
He wiped my tears.
"I'm sorry as Heaven cries for you."
"Life takes years."

"You deserve what love can bring."
"We want Heaven to sing."
"The Devil tries to take you from me!"
"Why would you love someone like that eternally?"

(Chorus)

Well my heart will still beat.
The sun will break the dawn.
Heaven falls to lift me,
to help me carry on.

Lost for Words

(Chorus) 1

Girl: I was lost for words,
way too long.
So to apologize,
I wrote you a song.

We've never missed a day.
We've never missed a night.
As hard as love got,
love stayed in sight.

From the beginning till now, every delicate touch,
turns me upside down. Even though I fight it, I miss it so much.

(Chorus) 2

Guy: I was lost for words,
way too long.
So to accept your apology,
I love your song.

Girl: I tried so hard to sail away.
I tried every day,
to push you away.

I put thoughts of negativity in your soul,
but I never could let you go.

Your love was so thick.
I felt it was a trick.

You are so forgiving and understanding,
I can't believe love is still happening.

(Chorus) 1

I was lost for words,
way too long.
So to apologize.
I wrote you this song.

Guy: I went from gentle to a violent streak.
Thank God for us,
the answer I knew in His words,
I knew what to seek.

Please understand,
I was lost for words.
Thank you for writing this song.

(Chorus) 2

I was lost for words,
way too long.
So to accept your apology,
I love your song

Girl: I never want to feel this hate again.
Baby, you're my love till the end.

(Chorus) 1

I was lost for words,
w-a-y too long.
So to apologize
I wrote you this song.

Both: Now let's finalize our abuses,
for they only were for love.

105

Definitions of love were so mixed up,
God had to fix it up.
Remember we asked for each other and how to love.
We both asked above.

We have love.
We have love.
We have l-o-v-e.

We have love, communication, respect, and all,
now that our words our found.
Know I never wanted to lose you at all.
The Lord won't let us fall.

(Chorus) 3

We were lost for words, way too long.
Here's our apology, this song.

W-e h-a-v-e l-o-v-e
F-r-o-m a-b-o-v-e

Rip It

As I dress with my best fads
to seek a good time at the bar.
I'm so excited to meet whoever you are.

Slick in my Porsche down the street,
preparing to groove with the beats.

I get into the club and order my first drink.
So many women, I couldn't think.

Blondes, brunettes, red and black hair.
So many women, it seems so unfair.

Then she caught my eyes across the dance floor.
Now it was time to take the tour

Chorus:

I'm gonna rip it.
I'm gonna twist it.
I'm gonna whip it.
I'm gonna rip it.

We grooved so close.
She smelled and felt and looked so good.

As hours passed, we left to my crib.
It's almost time to rip it.

We get in the door and kiss like strangers.
Toughing detours, hitting the majors.

I started unbuttoning her blouse and ripped it off.
She did the same and more for us to get into it.

Chorus

It's time to rip it.
It's time to twist it.
It's time to whip it.
It's time to rip it.

So sexy, so hot, so soft all over.
She tasted like a flower.

We got kinky in every way we could,
did things we never would.

I made her scream.
We came over and over again.
Tonight you're my girlfriend.

As we go our separate ways and kiss goodbye,
I said come over any time and get with it.
Baby, any time you want we'll rip it.

I'm gonna rip it.
I'm gonna twist it.
I'm gonna whip it.
I'm gonna rip it. 2X

Rip it
Rip it
Rip it Rip it

I'm gonna rip it.

Shared

(Chorus)

I wish we'd never shared our lives with someone else.
I wish I met you first in my life.
I wish you were always my wife.

I missed the times we could have shared.
You are the only one who cared.
I would have always been your teddy bear.

I'm jealous of your past.
My life wasn't fast.

It took a long time to meet you,
and you needed me too.

Why, oh why did I waste my time.
When you were mine…

(Chorus)

I wish we'd never shared our lives with someone else.
I wish I met you first in my life.
I wish you were always my wife.

You're so beautiful.
You are so for me.
Why couldn't I wait and see?

Instead I married at an early age,
had three kids that don't want to read the next page.

Now it's one or all,
but you were still hurting, still in a fall.
Introduced improperly, it wasn't his fault.

Deep down inside you're a great mom!
The best woman I've seen.
Sharing with her is a never ending dream.
I wish our children could see.
I'd share all of it with you and me.

(Chorus)

I wish we'd never shared our lives with someone else.
I wish I met you first in my life.
I wish you always were my wife.

At least we did get one more chance at sharing.
I'm your husband and you're my wife.
I'm just sorry for not sharing with you before,
We both were hurt and abused and used.
Now I'm proud we get to share our life.

(Chorus)

I wish we'd never shared our lives with someone else.
I wish I met you first in my life.
I wish you always were my wife.